Earth Tones

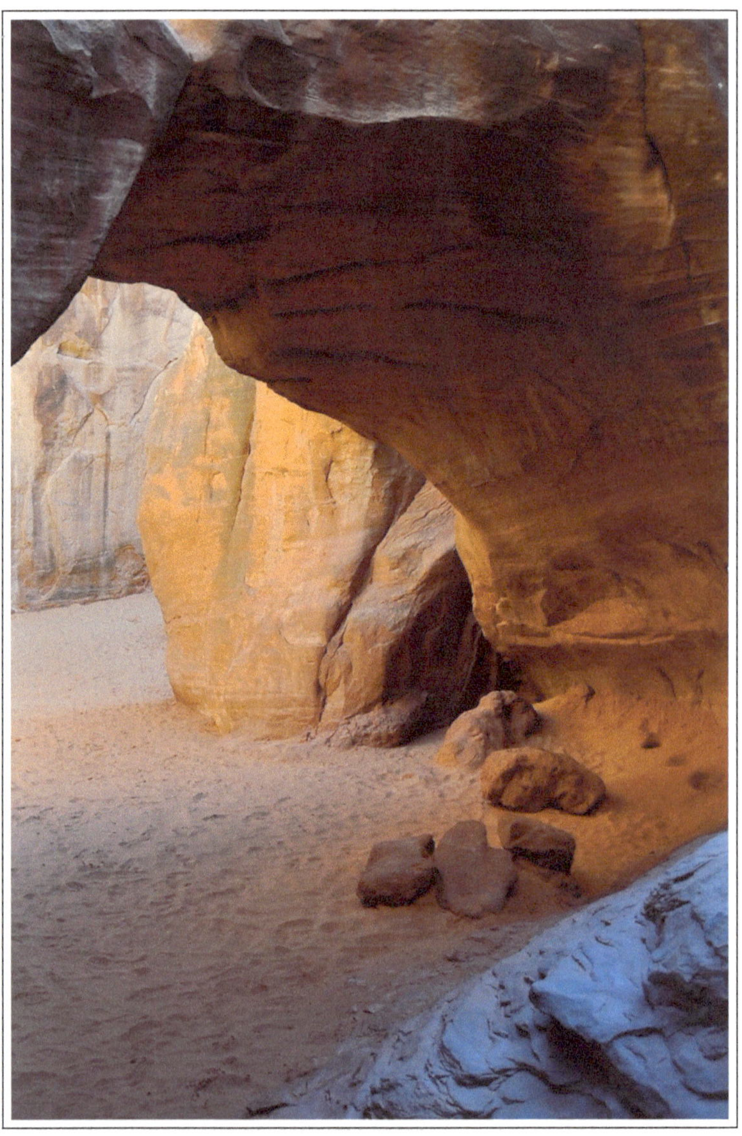

Earth Tones

Photographs & Poems
by DAVE PRUETT

ALBA ENTERPRISES LLC
Harrisonburg, Virginia
2020

Earth Tones

Publisher Cataloging-in-Publication Data

Pruett, Dave (Charles David), 1948 –
Earth Tones / Dave Pruett
ISBN: 978-0-578-68720-9 (Paperback)
1. POETRY / General
2. PHOTOGRAPHY / General
3. NATURE / General

Typeset by the author using the MEMOIR *class of* LaTeX.
Front and back cover designs by the author.
All photographs by the author.

ISBN: 978-0-578-68720-9 (Paperback)

Printed on demand by IngramSpark.

To Jill Moses
    whose poetry class primed the pump

To Charlie Finn
    kindred spirit—for poetic inspiration

To John Yungblut and Sun Eagle
    who opened my heart to see

And to Suzanne and Elena
    beloved women
    who've shared many adventures
    from whence these images

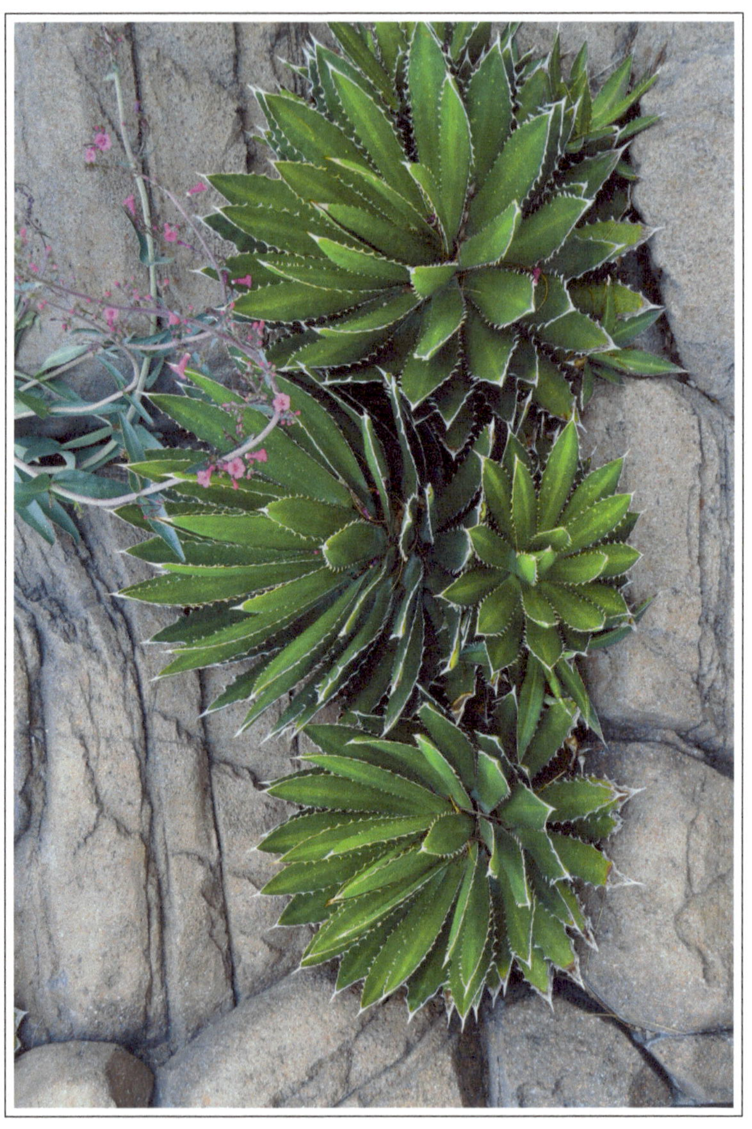

Contents

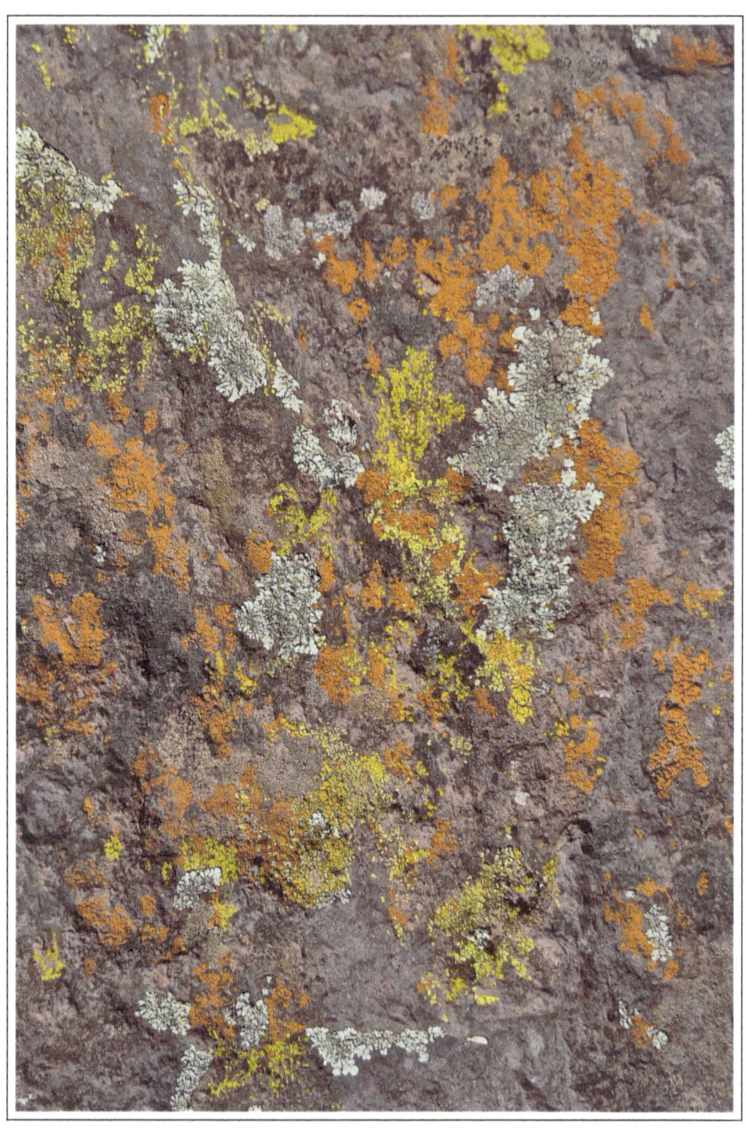

Preface

Photographers and poets are kindred spirits. The duty of each is to see; that is, to see what most fail to see. In the words of Russian artist Wassily Kandinsky:

> Everything that is dead quivers. Not only the things of poetry, . . . but even a white trouser button glittering out of a puddle in the street. . . . Everything has a secret soul, which is silent more often than it speaks.[1]

Photographers and poets, good ones, unveil the hidden soul of the subject, be that rock idol or trouser button.

Years ago, Michele, a friend and poet, unwittingly laid bare the bond between photography and poetry. Five years previously, while a graduate student at the University of Arizona, I'd gone backpacking on the Havasupai Indian Reservation, which adjoins the Grand Canyon. The inner sanctum, the village of Supai, is accessible only by helicopter or ten-mile trek through Havasu Canyon. To spare weight, I'd left at home my hefty 35mm camera. The day after our arrival, we hiked to Havasu Falls, where I experienced a scene of grandeur that has haunted me since. How I wanted a camera in that evanescent moment! Years later, tired of me bemoaning the lost photo op, Michele proffered sage advice: Write a poem. I did, and it's the title poem of this small volume. That act transformed a regret into gratitude.

Which then is better: to have a magical moment burned into synapses or onto film? Let the reader decide.

---

[1]Russian artist Wassily Kandinsky, cited in C.G. Jung, *Man and His Symbols*, New York: Dell Publishing Company, 1968, p. 292.

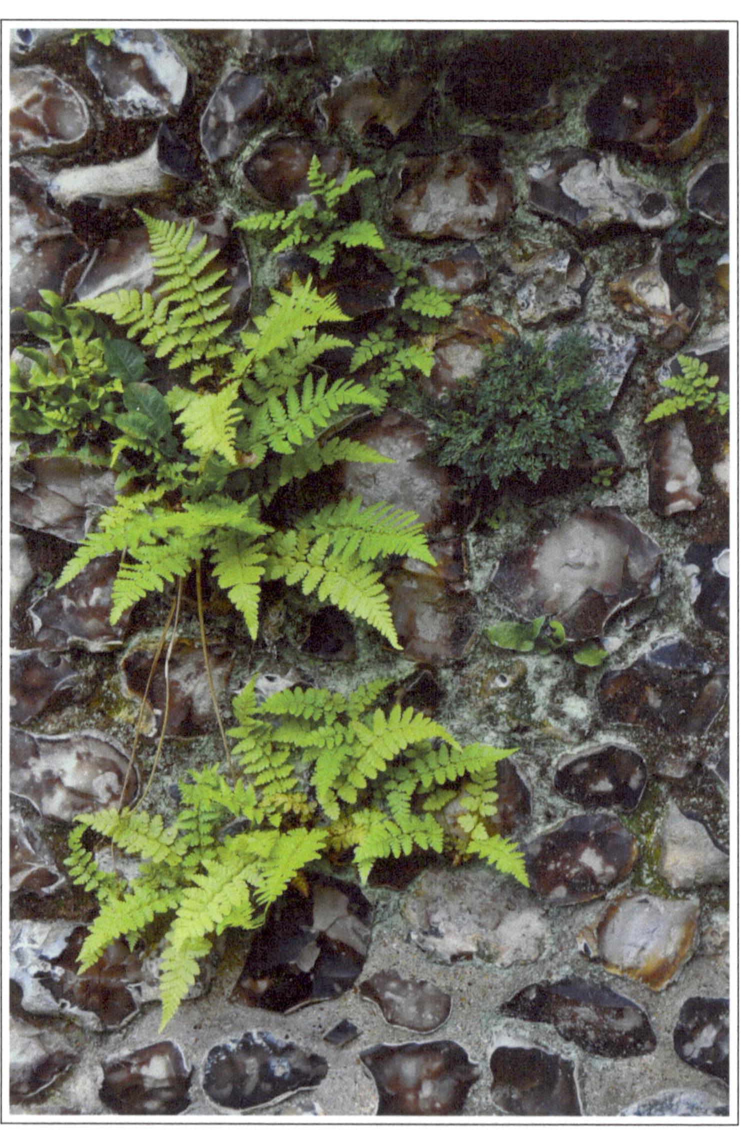

Centering

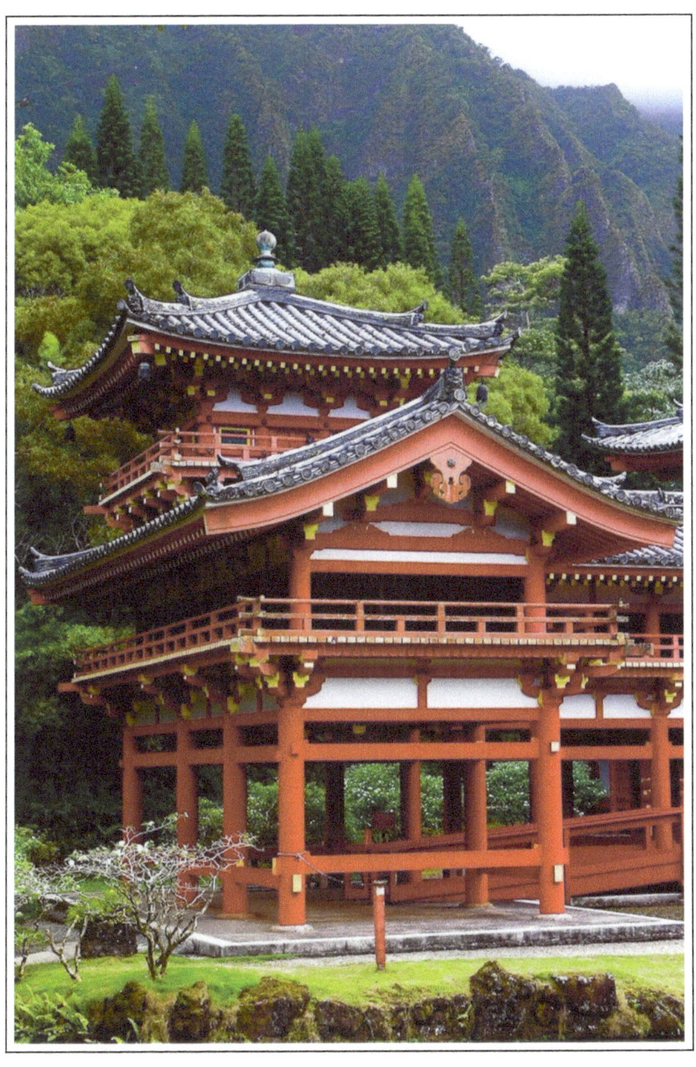

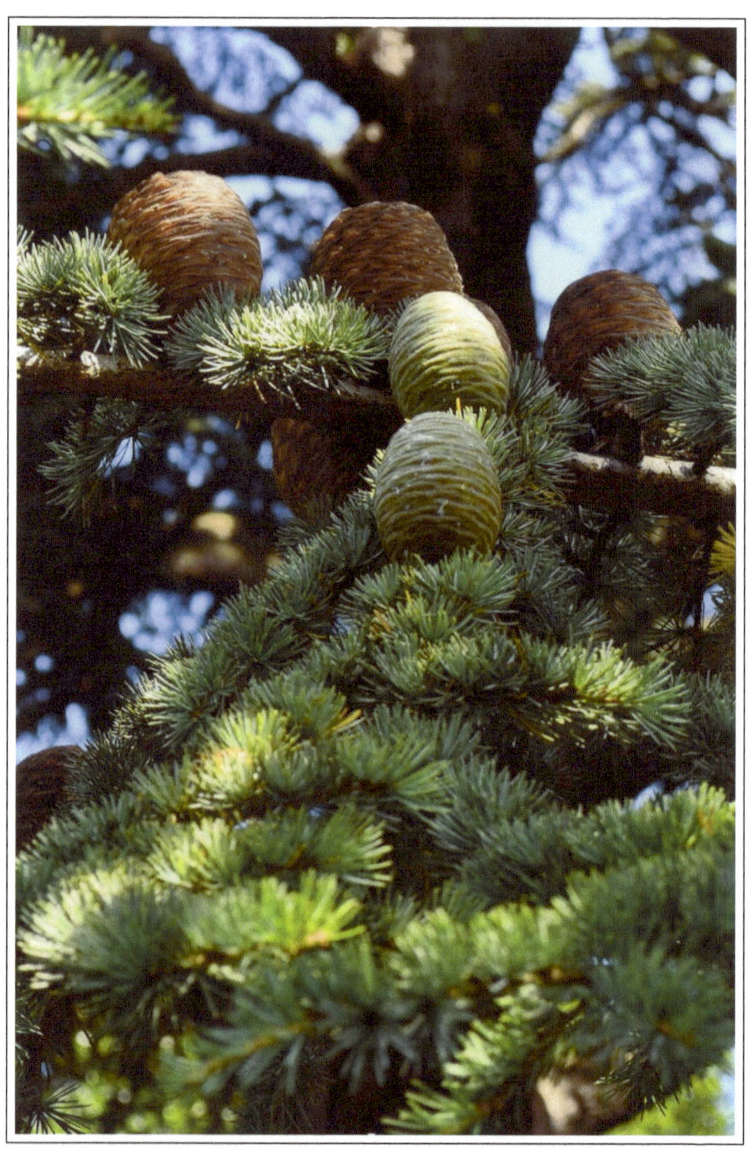

Contemplation (2006)

It's time again
for contemplation
the sharp thorn
in my meditation practice
So hard, so very hard
just to be present

The object of contemplation
an ordinary pine cone
kidnapped two years ago
from the east bank
of the Hudson
I twirl it round and round
in and out of soft focus
From every angle
seed whorls form
Fibonacci sequences
There is no angle
devoid of pattern or beauty
On warm days
the cone still bleeds
the pine-tar scent I love
But that too is judgment
Presence, mere presence

Today the cone arches
with arthritis
and conforms to the curve
of my cupped left hand
which spoons the cone
as do my wife and I
in morning and evening ritual
Before long the cone
is more than ordinary cone
and I am more than me

Breaking into thought
I ponder: Should I free
my contemplation captive
and send it home
to its carpeted woods
along the Hudson
to spawn a mighty pine
or perhaps a forest?

Yet more likely, might
my contemplation guide
liberate me, spirit becalmed,
to grow into a worthy man?

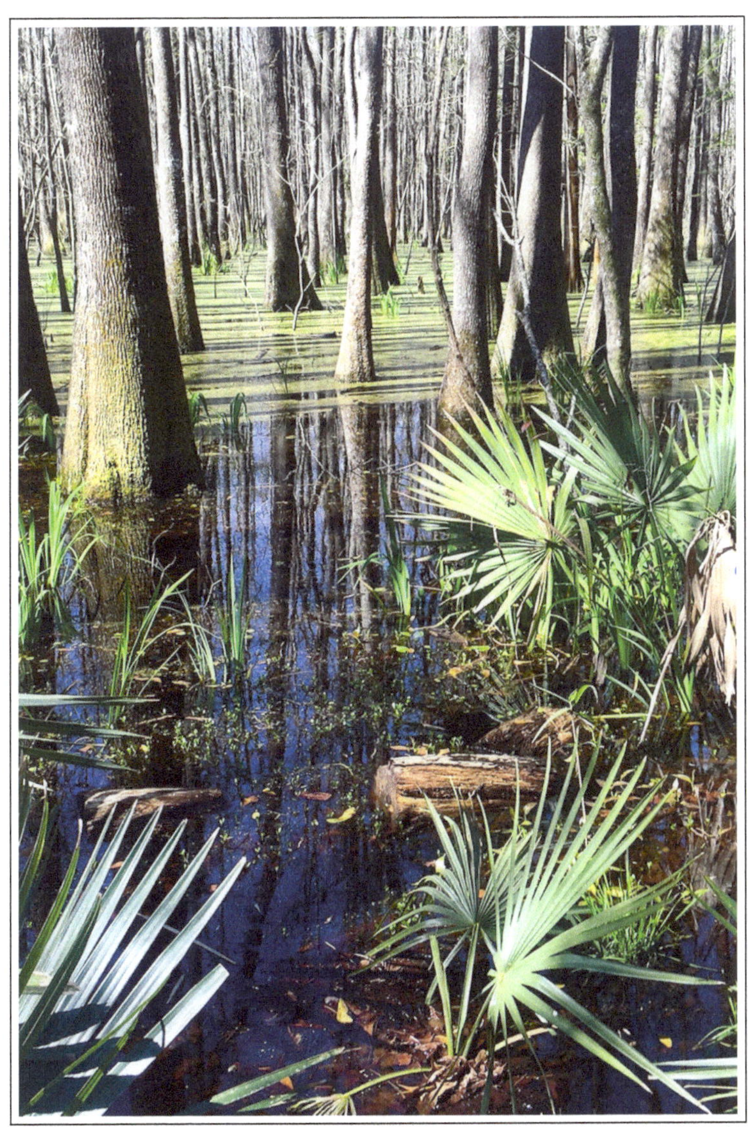

Ungrounded (1990)

At ten miles a minute
I hurdle above cotton sea,
chasing the red band
between bright heaven
and dull earth.
A child giggles across the aisle.
Somewhere behind, another cries.
Snatches of conversation
drift about the cabin like smells.
I hear words but no meaning.
Content to observe
but not participate,
I recall that summer eve in 1970.
Propelled by the merest wisp of wind,
we glided noiselessly
past the houses along the canal,
unrecognized, unnoticed,
as the voices from flickering TV's
and the squeals of children
floated our way
on the smoke of backyard grills
like the thoughts that flit
from flower to flower
before unworried sleep.

Now, wedged like a foot in a shoe,
I have again cast my soul upon air,
but I know the weight of neither.
As the red band burns dim
joining darkness to darkness,
I wonder: Does spirit float on air?

"Are you getting off in Dallas?" I ask
breaking the silence, thinking
perhaps two souls are lighter than one.

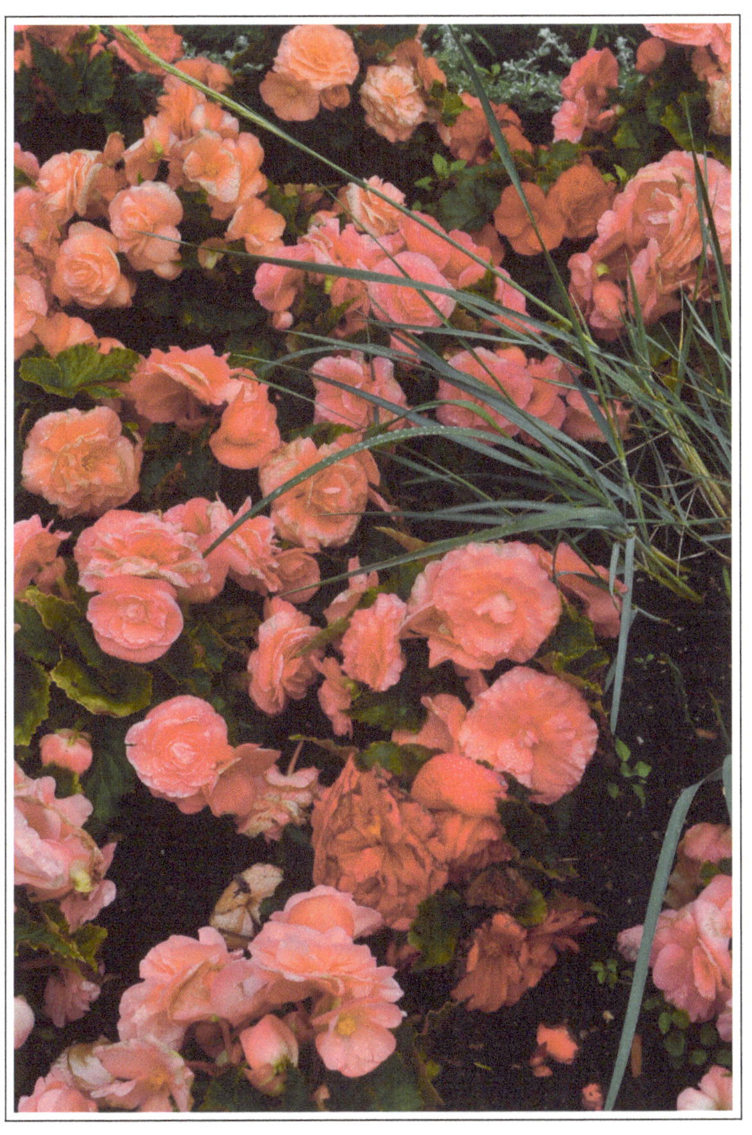

Grandma Sheila (1990)

You've aged ten years
in the last one,
your face as deeply lined
as an apple doll.
Your body has wasted
to nothing but loose folds
clinging to a worn and bent frame,
all the weight
a battered heart can bear.

It's hard to believe
you spent a lifetime plump.
Your hair is the purest white
and plastered down.
For so long you kept it
dyed jet-black
and always cared for.
But the fire in your eyes
has not dimmed.

When we saw you in January,
we thought it farewell.
I'm glad we were wrong.
Still, second partings
are always awkward,
as though the heart
can bear its nakedness
no more easily than excess.

On that day
we soaked in your every word
as an August earth
soaks up an April rain.
You told us of Dad
and the precious eggs.

Of Bill's first cigar.
Of times so tough
you and Granddaddy didn't eat
until the kids were full.
Of "Pot" the dog,
—Daddy couldn't say "Spot"—
over whom he and Billy cried
for three solid days
until you and Granddaddy
drove all the way
to North Side
to beg him back
from the colored man
you'd given him to.
And how the little dog,
on seeing the boys,
took a flying leap,
landing in the open model-T
reeking of skunk,
before the car
had even rolled to a halt.

And how we Pruett's
came by the cabin.
Exhausted and frazzled
by work and family,
on the verge of nervous collapse,
you had gone to Charlottesville
to see a specialist.
"Mrs. Pruett," Dr. Thomason said,
"you've got to take a month off
from responsibilities
and get away."
"I can't do that, Dr. Thomason,
We're not wealthy people,"
you'd said, and returned
to Bluefield no better.

On a Sunday afternoon drive
across the mountain
the FOR SALE sign
had set you thinking,
maybe there, close to home,
you could get the prescribed rest.
It was out of the question
Granddaddy reminded you.
Money was so scarce.
Yet you'd gone to the banker
without Granddaddy knowing
and told him your story.
"Mrs. Pruett," he'd said,
"I don't know you from Adam,
but I'm going to give you the loan."

When Granddaddy found out,
he thought you'd lost your mind,
and maybe you had,
but we still have the cabin,
and we still have you.

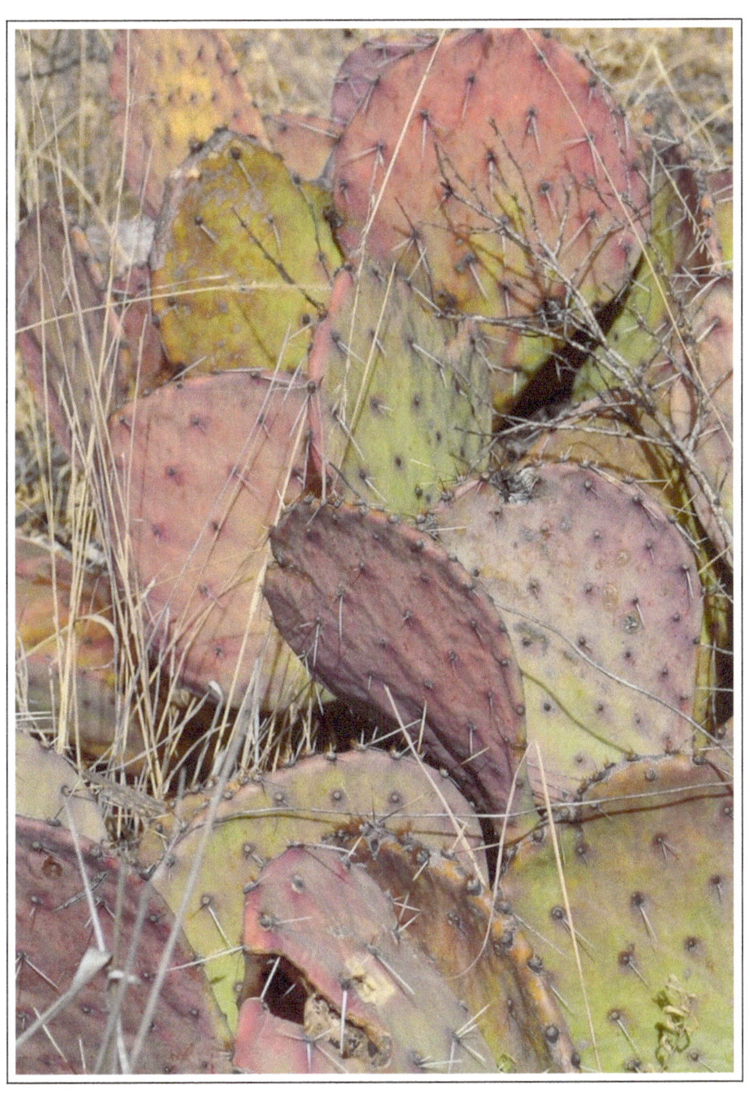

Father, Son (1991)

The Doctor

Flattered, he had protested mildly
that there was nothing to see
but a shabby, junk-filled office.
Still, she had come to meet the family
and would not be dissuaded,
and so the visit was arranged,
around noon, when he often
skipped lunch for a cat nap.
Shortly after twelve, the nurse
beckoned us through the door
to the tiny inner sanctum
where a steel-eyed man
sat open-necked, gold-chained,
and salt-and-pepper haired
behind a cluttered desk, beneath
the gaze of approving diplomas.
Entombing the desk, bookshelves
on four walls disgorged their
manila-wrapped secrets,
the confessions of half a town's
population to the crimes of
diabetes, hypertension, and
spinal meningitis.

Amidst the manila and sheepskin,
amidst the professional samples,
in every nook and cranny,
spilling off the desk top,
the plaques, the pictures,
the knick-knack offerings
of a community's grateful people
to its healer God.

The Son

The man behind the desk grinned
his jack-o-lantern grin
and rose to greet us.
And as he stood
his five-foot-four
towered over my five-foot-ten,
and I was six-years old
and by his side
on the elevator
where I wondered about
the bell-tones:
What could they mean?
And tall men with white coats
entered in, stethoscopes
dangling about their necks
while stooped men in green coats
wheeled out their carts
at every floor.

And then the doors flung open
and then we were walking
ever silently down the endless
Listerine-scented corridor,
ever silently,
save for the click-clack echoes
of big shoes swallowing whole
the clatter of little ones.

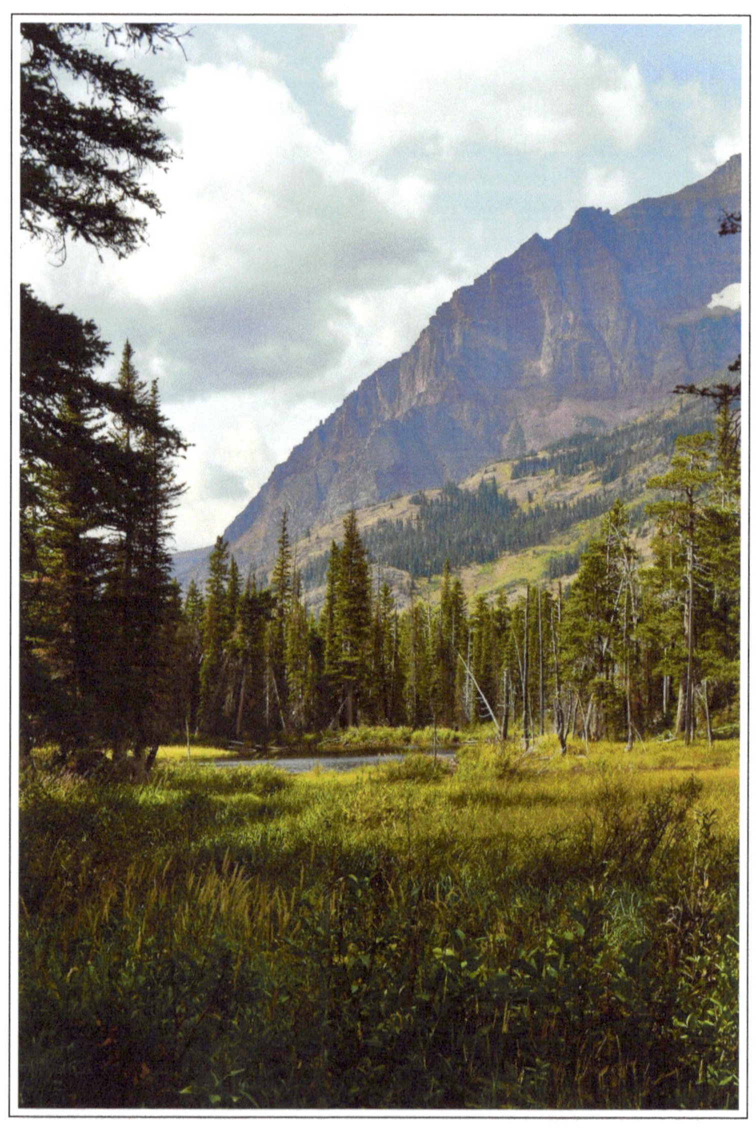

Dew glistens
on the sinuous,
sleek, sulking
panther poised
in tensed power
heart pounding
in pulsing thunder
it sinks soundless
into shadow
undisrupted,
the dank, dark dignity
of ferned forest.

No breeze stirs
the humming,
    buzzing,
        sigh
of musty earth,
or the enveloping
stillness.

At the careless blink
it will spring,
a blinding,
blurry fury
unleashed.

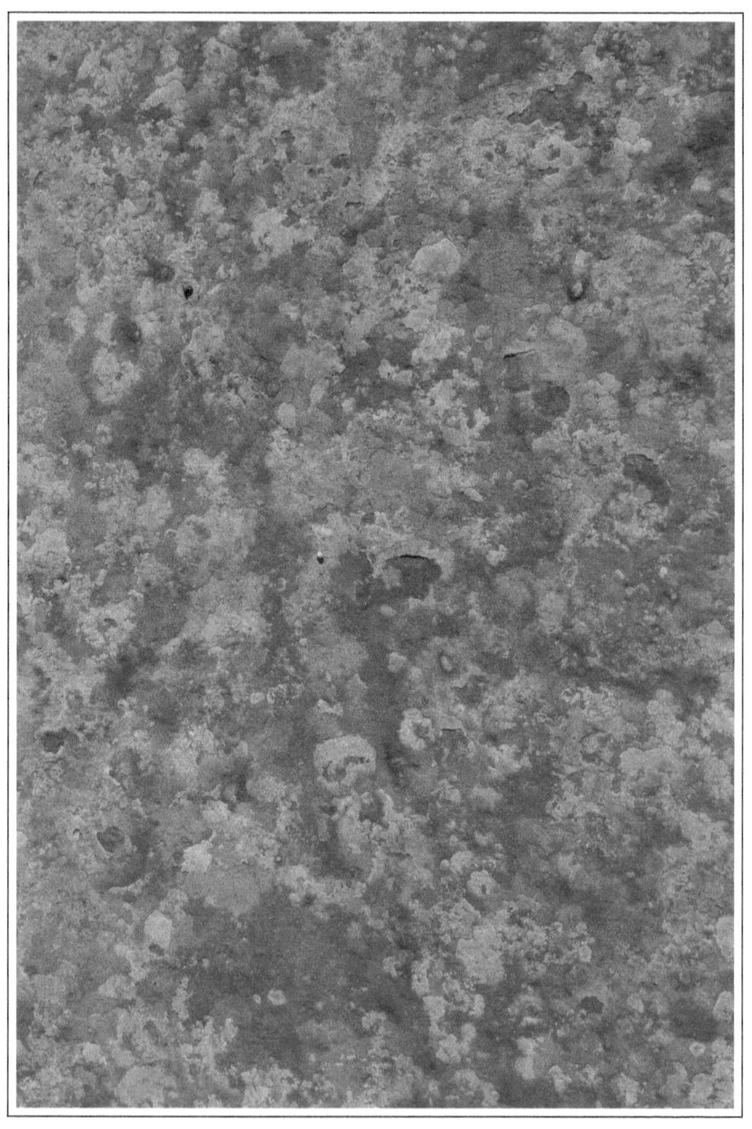

Tenure (1988)

Something in me recoils
at the 'respectability' of it all.
Seven colleagues up for tenure.
Seven careers form but two lines.
Thumbs up: "You're one of us."
Thumbs down: to the gas chambers.

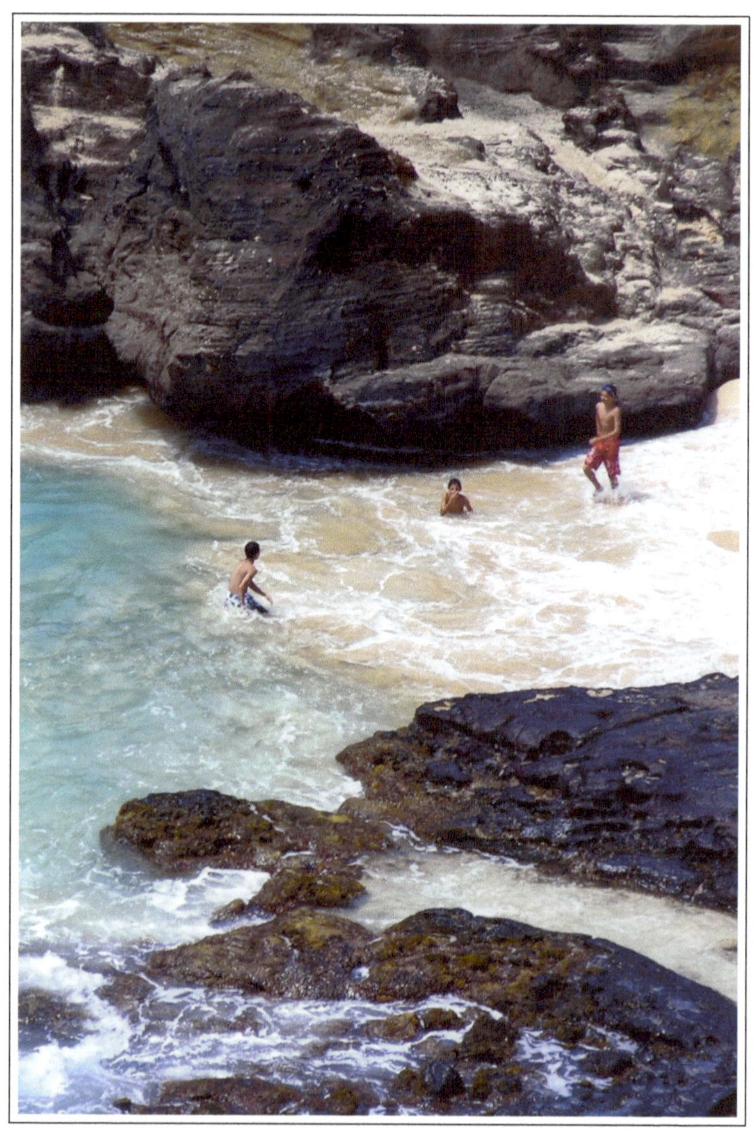

Psalm of Resolution (1988)

Like flotsam
have I ridden the breakers
tossed to and fro
unable to choose
the shelter of Mother shore
or the perils of Father deep.
Scientist or poet,
who shall I be?
Shall I trade in dreams or logic?
Shall I act from heart or mind?

Why choose white or black?
My ancestors roamed
among hills called Cherokee
and I will follow their ancient lead.
Mind and spirit have no quarrel
nor scientist and poet.
Two tongues will I make my own:
one language of dreams
another of reason.
As notes in harmony
will my words be spoken.
My soul will embrace both its parents
and I will be whole.

The civil strife will cease its sting
and the mixed blood will run deep
and rich and red.

Grounding

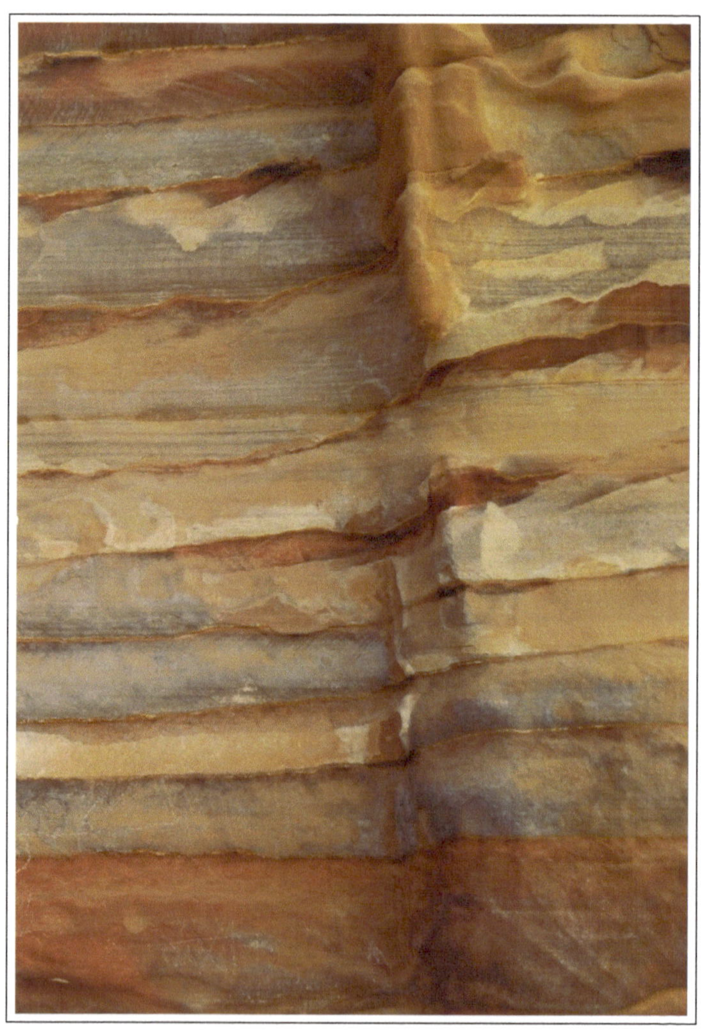

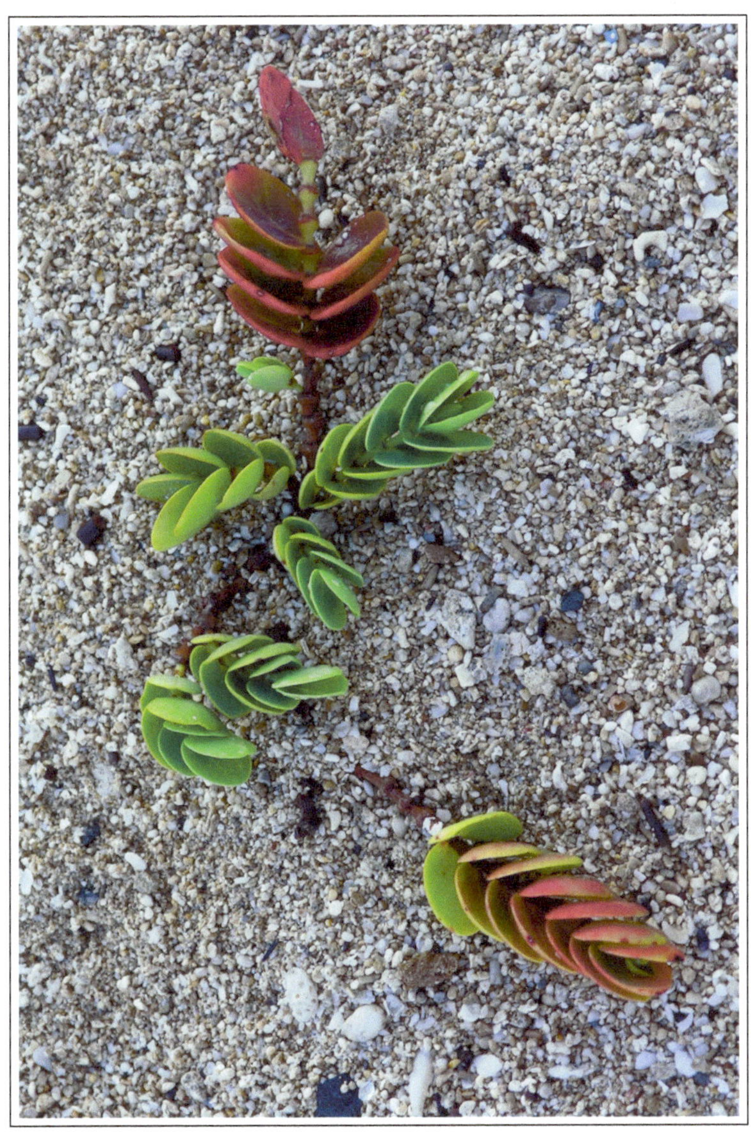

Womb (1991)

The Good Book says
of dust are we born
and to dust shall we return.
It is not so.
To dust we may return,
yet of water are we born.
Only he whose brow
has never crusted,
only she whose tears
are never tasted,
only we who never licked
the freshly opened wound
can doubt from whence we come.

I lie in semi-conscious bliss,
cradled by warm sand.
The waves sing lullabies
to the rhythm of my breath.
The wind and sun
massage my limbs.
My cares loft
on the wings of gulls
who laugh
and toss them into the sea.
Ticks of time drown
in roiling surf,
beats forever stilled.

I have swum for countless ages;
I have crawled for countless more.
In exhaustion I have washed ashore,
freshly cast from salty womb
to lie among shells.

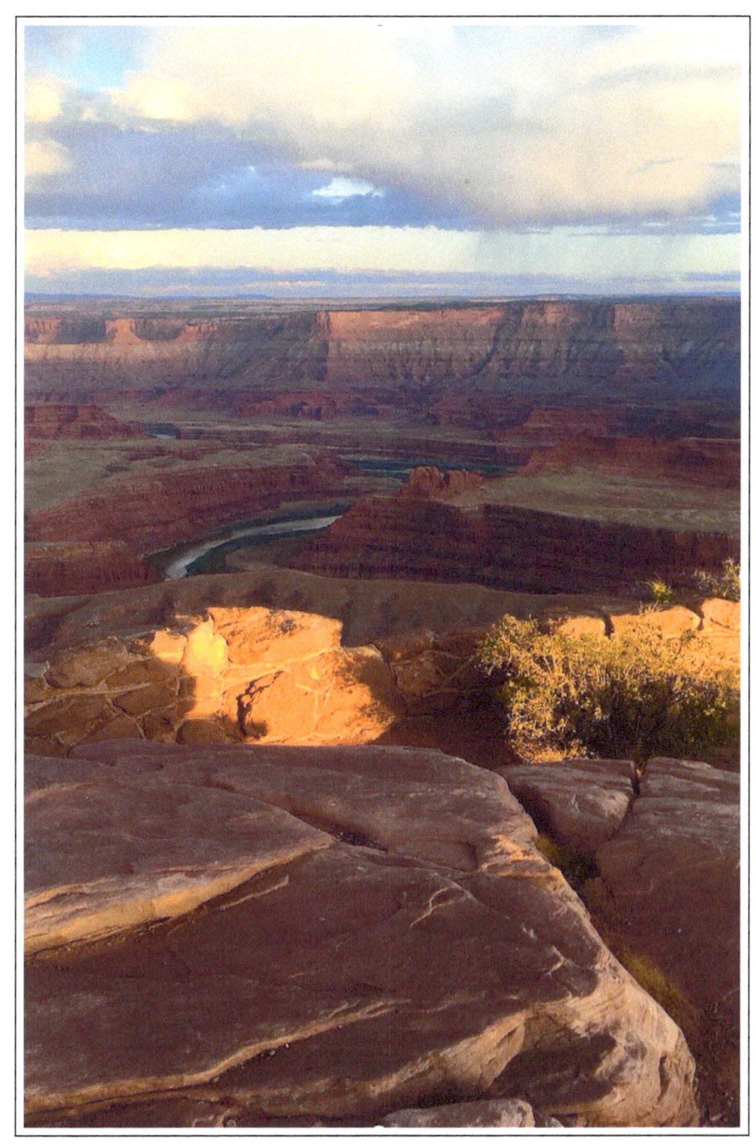

Earth Tones (1989)

Colors
earth tones mostly
Red man
bare-chested and pony-tailed
astride a bay mare
belly deep
in a pool of blue-green
the horse's
    graceful
        motion
            silent
against the roar
of the water's
    hundred-
        foot
            drop
over red travertine

Canopied
by a sky of cloudless blue
        Lost
among canyon walls
of reds and yellows
so damned high
impenetrable I'd swear
had I not descended
on blistered feet
into that Holy of Holies
whose mists soothe
the desert-parched
deep in green shade

Five years have passed
Still I see
the half-naked man
on silent horse
and the colors:
　　earth tones
　　　　mostly

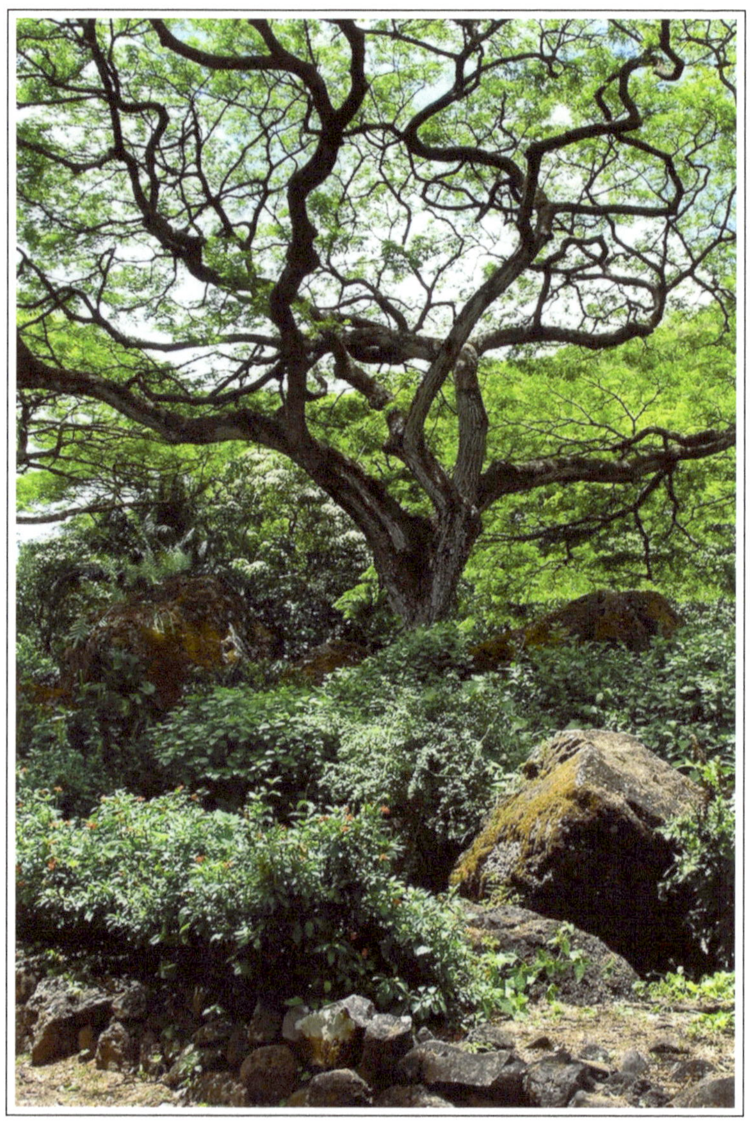

We tread the first October leaves
along a fire road that clings
to the bank of a deep ravine
just above the creek.
It is three in the afternoon
and dusk along our path.
Tulip poplars line each bank.
Like soldiers at attention
they stand clean cut and tall.
Chins held high, their faces
glow in the slant-light
while shadows submerge
their black boots.

The philodendron and I play a game.
I turn its back to the window
and tell it not to misbehave.
Like the school child made
to sit in the corner,
it pretends to obey.
But in an instant not quite glimpsed,
it whirls again to face the sun.

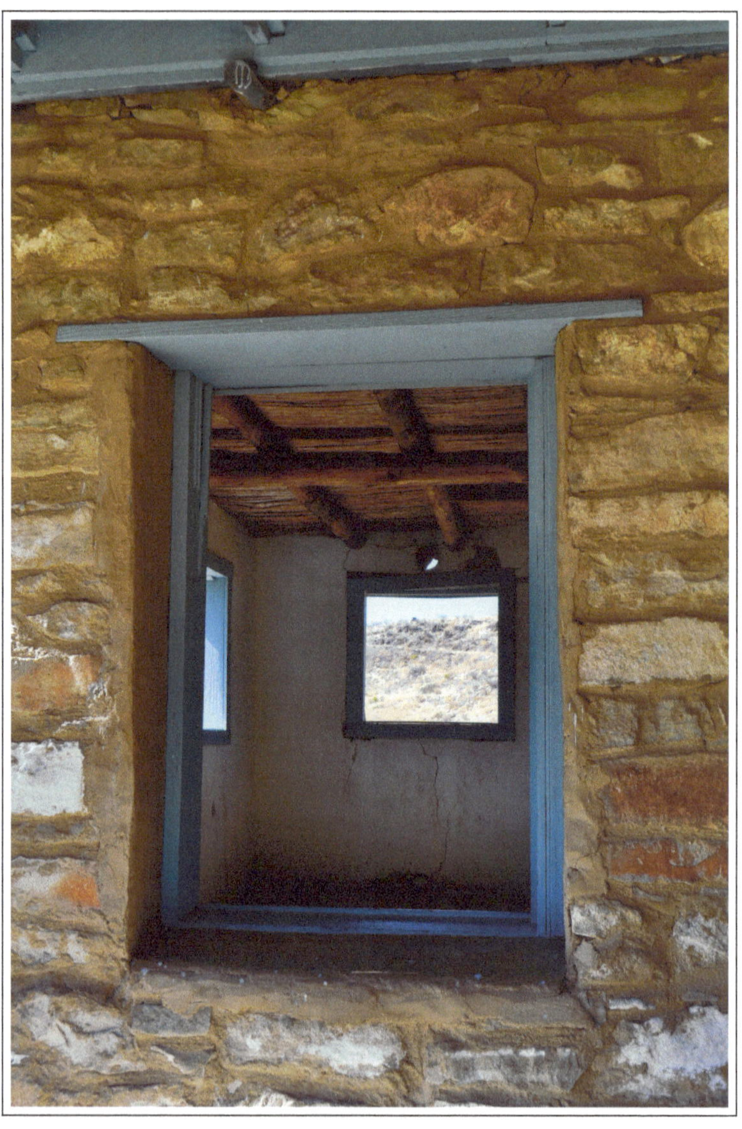

Beyond the Milky Way (1990)

A billion stars
blink yellow
in a sky of green.
Like a universe
in continual creation,
constellations coalesce
and dissolve
before our eyes,
fleeting Cassiopeia,
aging Aquarius.

We halt our journey.
What sailor can reckon
when the stars
have minds
of their own?

Dark maples
at the edge of the wood
frame two sides of a field
where sweet summer mists
cling low to the ground,
obscuring the apparitions
beyond the firefly Milky Way.
We douse the headlamps,
and letting our eyes adjust
to the light of dusk,
conjure seven brown forms,
deer, light years away.
Unaware of our presence,
or unconcerned,
they browse, heads down,
drunk on dewy grass.

Spellbound and immobile,
we watch apparitions
and Aquarius,
all that one can do
when one has lost fix
on the pole star.

The evening sky dims
then blackens.
Upon the wishing star
we take new bearing
and drive on.

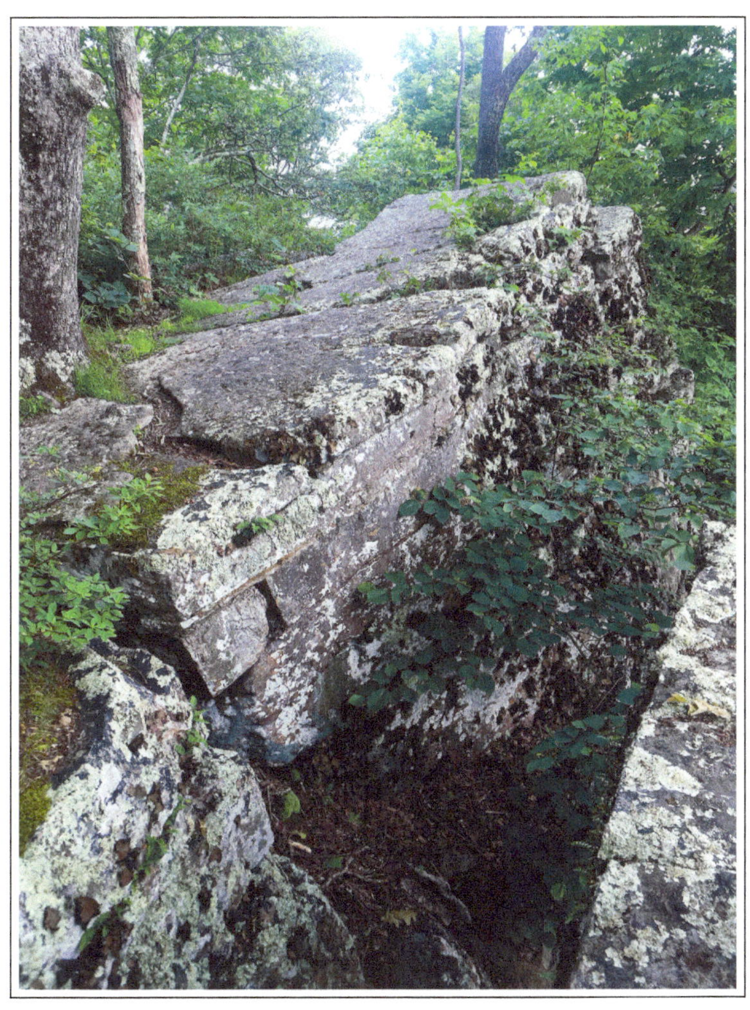

Appalachians (1987)

O Blue Ridge, Allegheny
You were once noble Teton
Or lofty Himalaya

Wrinkles now
Those once-proud features
Your wealth scattered
To the Earth's children
Your shadow softens each passing day
You while the hours stooped, quieted
Awaiting the ultimate letting-go
Pondering if in your stead
Some future sea will fill
Peak will rise
Or wheat field
Find its home

Youth in its quests
Looks beyond gentle summits
And youth in its hurry
Pauses not for quiet beauty
But having seen many come
And many go
You know Youth
And also Age
And understand them both
O ancient Appalachians

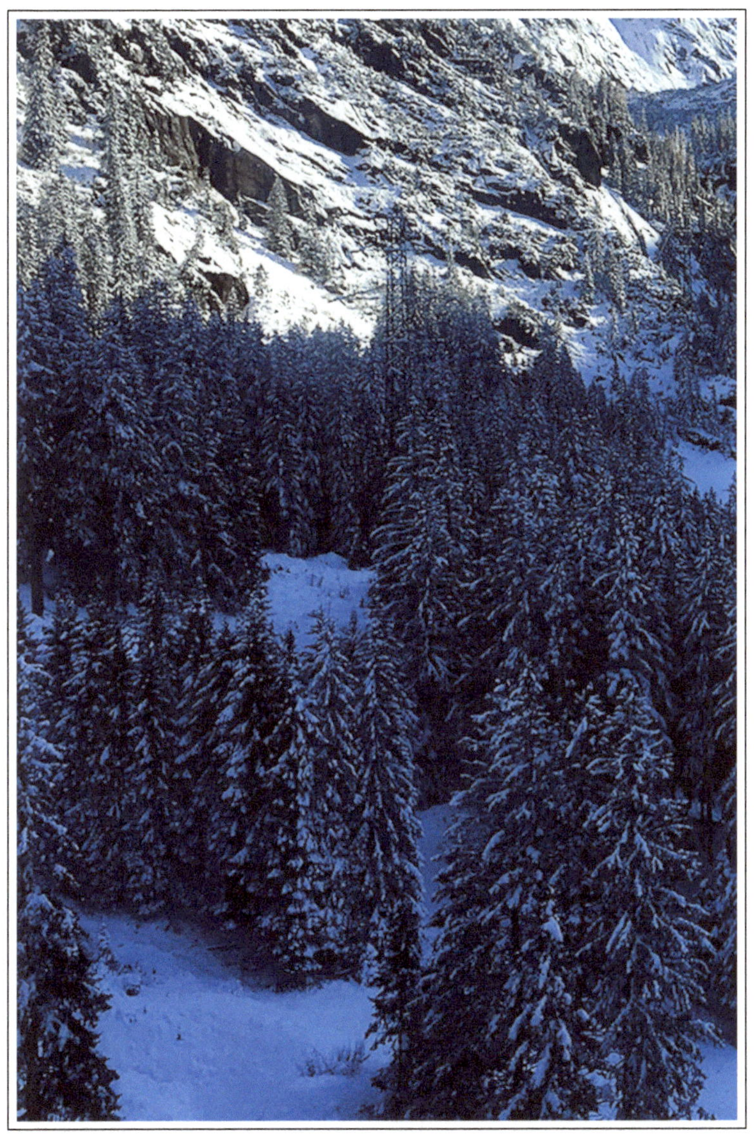

Arctic Fox (1993)

I am haunted by your image.
I cannot divert my eyes.
When the shutter shuddered,
did you sense your spirit diminished?
Did you recoil and scamper
like Amish children?

Like the red man offering prayer
over the pierced and still-quivering deer
I give thanks for that spirit stolen
to fix your essence
on the photographer's plate,
meat that now feeds my sedentary soul.

You do not move, yet my mind's eye
sees you bounding over brilliant snow,
shy white apparition, invisible
save for the shadow fluttering beneath
and the telltale lump of pitch
at the end of a perfect conical snout.
You pant on the run,
but the breaths die mid-stride
and cling as crystals to the fur
of your Zen-like lower lip.

For a moment my mind plays tricks
and I think back on years
in the Great Sonoran Desert
and on your distant cousin, Coyote
with his slinking gate
and his huge ears to cool
during blast-furnace days
and locate the faintest scurry-sound
in nocturnal prowls for prey.

But you do not slink
and your ears are but furred tufts
that barely protrude beyond
thick white fur combed radially
by unrelenting wind.
At the silent top of the earth
you sleep drift-snug by night
and hunt at daybreak
by keen sight and not by sound.

It is your eyes that haunt.
They are guileless and alien,
as alien as those in the artist's
rendering of a visitor from deep space.
And as wise—deep amber,
liquid and alert, they gaze
at a distant point and unblinkingly
reflect a blinding sun.

I have gazed long
at the serene intelligence
in your face, which one does
not find among the two-legged.
If ever I doubted whether
the creatures have souls,
I doubt no more.

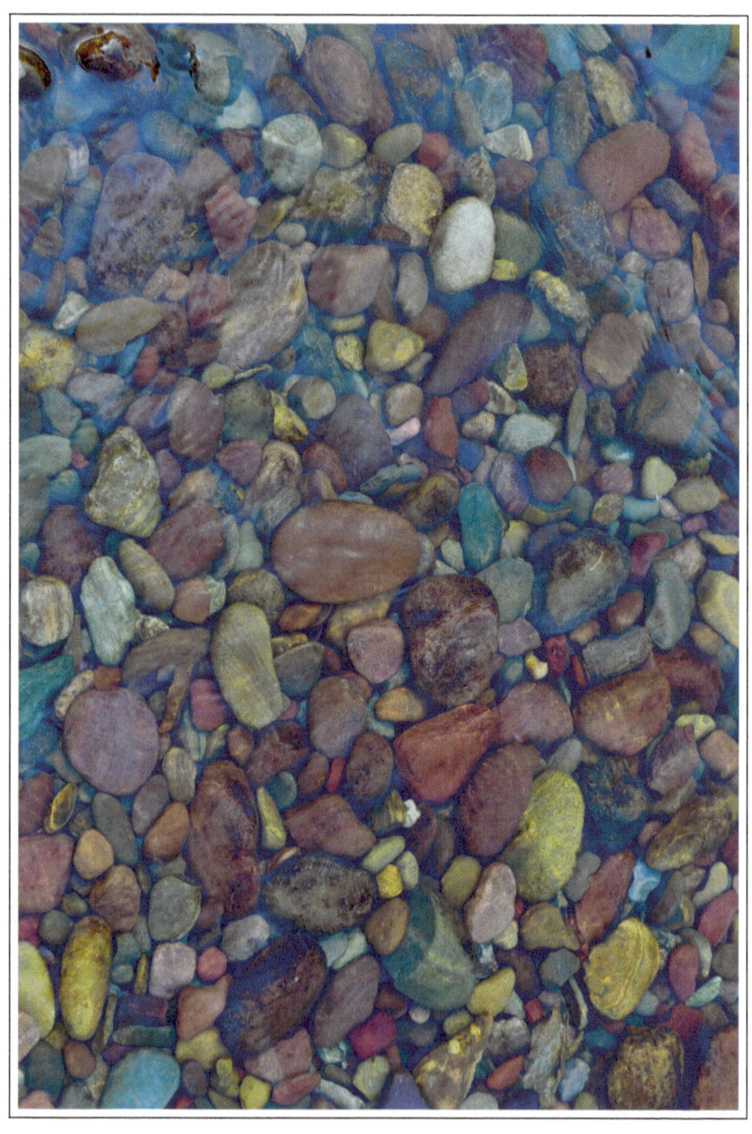

Cleansing Rain (1987)

Wrung from unclaimed Angst
sorrow's droplets
flow two together here
    three together there
mingle in rivulets of brine
and gather into flood

Windows of the soul turn liquid
burst forth in twin cascades
roaring, ROARing
    in moans and sobs
    in arms flailing
    in wails and whimpers
    in futile fury

Floodwaters rage
they churn, they muddy
they sweep up
along their course
the debris of lifetimes:
    dear losses
        ancient hurts
            fears no longer needed
a thousand cast-off garments

Fury spent
    flow ebbs
        rivulets wither
            soul sparkles
                becalmed
            afresh
        anew
    alive
alert

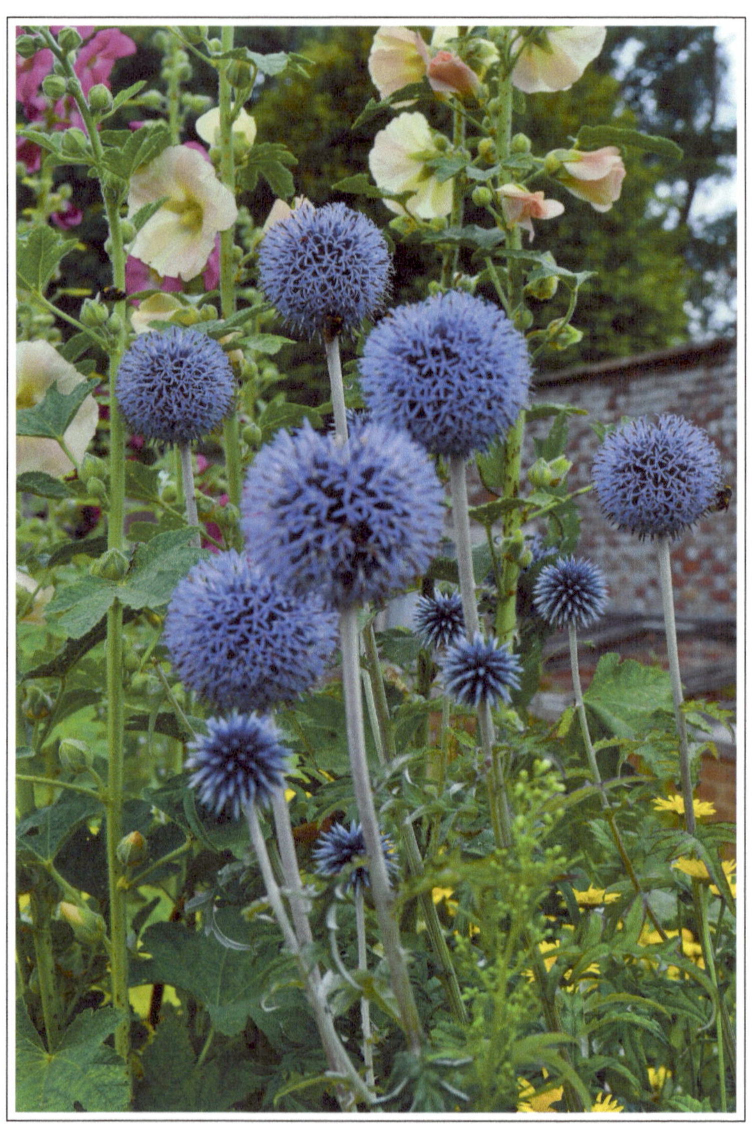

What a World Needs (2020)

"Gravity is Cool,"
the disarming title
of a whip-smart paper
by iconoclast physicist
Freeman Dyson.
I met him once, the
paper his parting gift

Gravity's cool
"spooky action
at a distance,"
mystifying even to Einstein,
tethers planets to their stars,
each Keplerian orbit
one beat of a celestial clock
ticking out the eons
of deep time,
while evolution slow cooks
its magical stew
on spaceship Earth
and most probably
on every other
Goldilocks wanderer
in one-hundred-billion
galaxies

But gravity runs hot too
when it crushes dying stars
igniting supernovae
that vaporize
suns ten times greater
than our own,
spewing carbon, oxygen, iron
even uranium
across light-years

of quantum froth
the stardust of which
I am knit together, and
you too are wrought
and the oak
and the shark
and the otter

What then does a world need?
Chaos, by God—
    and order,
Devastation—
    and rejuvenation,
Fleeting creativity—
    and fathomless drudgery,
a pinch of the former,
a neutron-star tablespoon
of the latter,
both the legacy of
gravity's cosmic dance,
the core sacrificial act
of a universe's
ceaseless labor
to flower beings
sufficiently awake
to enjoy the show,
though not yet awake enough
to thank our lucky stars
or treasure this shining orb
called home

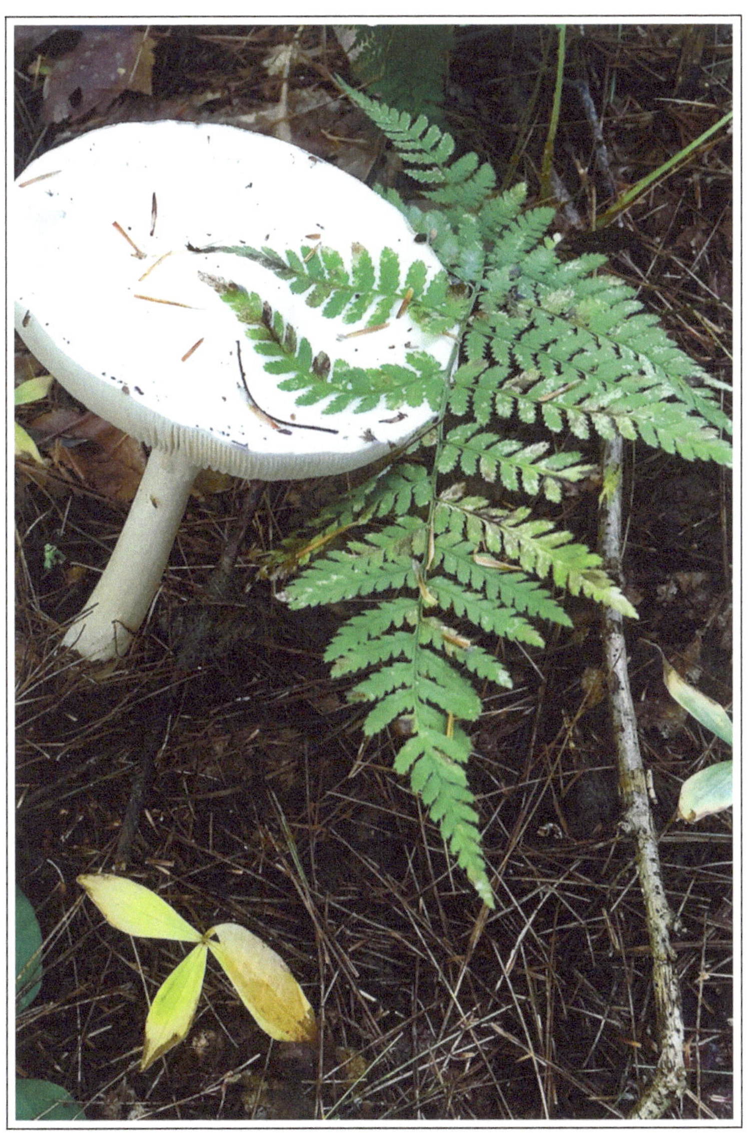

Prayer of Gratitude (2007)

This prayer was inspired by two cherished mentors, both now gone to spirit world: Sun Eagle, Mattaponi "wisdomkeeper;" and John Yungblut, Episcopalian priest turned Quaker.

>O Great Spirit
>>I am grateful for another day of life
>>And another day closer to death
>>Whenever that day comes,
>>May it be a good day to die
>>And may I make a good end

>O Great Spirit
>>I am grateful for a night of rest
>>And a day of labor
>>May my rest be of the pure in heart
>>And my labor not be in vain

>O Great Spirit
>>I am grateful for my friends,
>>Who see what is good in me
>>And for my enemies, who keep me alert
>>May I live in the wisdom
>>That turns enmity toward friendship

>O Great Spirit
>>I am grateful for the light within me
>>And for that which is dark also
>>May I not hide what is light
>>May I make peace with what is not

>O Great Spirit
>>"Giver of all good gifts,
>>Give me but one thing more:
>>A grateful heart,"[2] a grateful heart

---

[2]The short prayer that graced every meal shared with John.

List of Images

NOTE: All photographs in this volume were taken by the author using digital cameras: a Nikon D5000, an Olympus C8080, or an iPhone SE, in order of prevalence.

About the Author

DAVE PRUETT is a retired computational scientist and academic applied mathematician. He has a decade of experience in the aerospace industry at NASA Langley Research Center and nearly three decades of teaching mathematics in Virginia: at Virginia Commonwealth University, the College of William and Mary, and James Madison University (JMU).

While a full-time faculty member in the Department of Mathematics and Statistics at JMU, Dave garnered a number of teaching awards including the first Mengebier Endowed Professorship and the first Provost's Award for Excellence in Honors Teaching, the latter for a groundbreaking honors course that explores the interface between science and spirituality. In 2012 *Reason and Wonder*, his love letter to the cosmos and a spinoff of honors teaching, was published by Praeger. The American Library Association honored *Reason and Wonder* with a Choice Award shortly following its publication.

In retirement, Dave has been section-hiking the Appalachian Trail and has a trail memoir in progress: *VAs' AT—Walking the Appalachian Trail in the Virginias*. Dave and his wife, Suzanne Fiederlein, live in Harrisonburg, in Virginia's central Shenandoah Valley. Suzanne currently directs JMU's Center for International Stabilization and Recovery (CISR). They have one daughter, Elena, a millennial.